AMINATA COOTE

God Is In Control

21 Devotions About the Sovereignty of God

HopeLight
Publishers

First published by Hopelight Publishers 2024

Cover design by Hopelight Graphics

First edition

ISBN: 978-976-8334-31-2

This book was professionally typeset on Reedsy.
Find out more at reedsy.com

To the woman seeking to submit her life to God, may God grant you the desire of your heart.

I know, Lord, that our lives are not our own. We are not able to plan our own course.

Jeremiah 10:23 NLT

Contents

Introduction

Hi Friend,

Thank you for picking up a copy of this devotional. Maybe you did so because you'd like to learn more about God's sovereignty. Or you're curious about what God's sovereignty means for your life.

In either case, I'm glad you're on this journey with me.

The Oxford Dictionary defines sovereign as supreme power or authority. When something is supreme, it is the greatest, best, or the highest authority.

The leader of a department or country expects certain behavior from the subordinates. Subordinates are to be respectful and use a polite tone when conversing. They should follow the instructions provided by their leaders.

As subordinates, we're assigned tasks to be completed according to the established standards. If not, there will be consequences, whether coaching or discipline.

The Bible urges us to acknowledge and submit to the leadership of our earthly rulers. So what about our Sovereign Lord?

When we say God is Sovereign, we mean He is the greatest and is above all things. However, we don't honor and respect God as He deserves.

This devotional will explore God's sovereignty and focus on answering three key questions:

1. What God's sovereignty means
2. Why God is Sovereign
3. How we should respond to God's sovereignty

I pray you'll complete these devotionals with renewed awe for our Sovereign Lord. I pray that praise for Jehovah will fill your heart until it brims over in worship.

Are you ready, girlfriend? It's time to learn more about the God we serve.

I

What God's Sovereignty Means

Let's explore what we mean when we say God is sovereign.

1

God Does What He Pleases

Psalm 115:3 NKJV — But our God is in heaven; He does whatever He pleases.

Every time I read this title, there's resistance in my spirit. Saying that God does what He pleases sounds selfish. But that's incorrect, right?

God is not selfish. Why does this verse make it sound like He is? Yet this phrase appears many times in the Bible, so let's explore what it means. Let us first acknowledge the character of God.

God is loving, merciful, long-suffering, just, compassionate, and kind. This is what God said about Himself in Deuteronomy 32:39:

> *See now that I, even I, am he, and there is no god with*
> *me: I kill, and I make alive; I wound, and I heal: neither*
> *is there any that can deliver out of my hand (KJV).*

God has ultimate power over life. He has ultimate power over death. God has the power to heal and the power to destroy. He makes these decisions based on His omniscient knowledge.

The Bible has many stories about men and kings who served pagan gods. Some of these kings even believed themselves to be gods. Where are those kings now?

We learn about some of them from archaeology finds and history lessons, but many of them have nothing recorded about them outside of the pages of the Bible.

Many would not have heard about Nebuchadnezzar, Cyrus, Asa, or Hezekiah without the accounts written about them in God's Word.

The same is not true about God. Since the beginning of time, there have always been those who testify about God's sovereignty. They tell of His might and power, reminding everyone that God is in control. He does as He pleases.

If God were as fickle as humanity, that would mean something different for us. It would mean tiptoeing around Him lest He destroy us all because He had a bad day.

But God is not like us, and while He does as He pleases, He does everything with our eternal salvation in mind.

Our God is in heaven. He does what pleases Him. He is also a God of love and mercy. His mercies are new every morning (Lamentations 3:22–23).

Because God does not lie, and His character is unchangeable, we can trust Him.

Prayer

Yahweh,

You are God over all things. You have the authority to do as You choose and the compassionate nature to do what is right. Help me accept that You have ultimate power. I submit my will into Your hands. In Jesus' name, Amen.

2

God's Purpose Will Not Be Thwarted

*Job 42:2 NIV — "I know that you can do all things; no purpose of
yours can be thwarted."*

The Book of Job started on a buoyant note:

*Job 1:1 NLT — There once was a man named Job
who lived in the land of Uz. He was blameless—
a man of complete integrity. He feared God and stayed
away from evil.*

We're then given a snapshot of Job's life. He was married with
ten children. He had cattle and servants and was the richest man
in his community (Job 1:2-3).

But if you read a lot of fiction or watch movies, you know
things couldn't continue on that positive trend. Otherwise,
what's the point?

Sure enough, by the end of the chapter, his children are dead
and so are his animals. The number of servants had significantly
dwindled.

By chapter two, Job's health is gone and his wife is encouraging him to curse God and die (Job 2:9).

Things couldn't get worse until his friends showed up and blamed Job for his problems.

Neither Job nor his friends were privy to the conversation between God and Satan, where God gave the devil permission to test Job (Job 1:6-12, 2:1-7)

In response to his suffering, Job demands an audience with the Lord and God grants it to him.

After listening to Job complain about what amounted to chapters in our Bibles, God had a lot to say.

God walked Job through the Creation story and expounded on His dominance over everything. Job's only response was to submit to God's sovereignty (Job 42:2).

There's a lesson here: we can complain, whine, resist, or quarrel, but God has ultimate power over our lives.

And that's wonderful. Just think, if it had been up to the devil, Job would have been dead at the first test, along with his family.

But the devil had to stay within the boundaries God had set. He could take Job's possessions, but not harm him physically (Job 1:12). Later, Satan could harm Job, but he couldn't take his life (Job 2:4-6).

Like Job, our lives and possessions are in God's hands. It is what God decides will happen. No one can thwart God's will. Let us revel in that.

Prayer

Adonai,

My life is in Your hands. I submit everything I have, everything I am, my present, and my future into Your hands. May Your will prevail in every area of my life. In Jesus' name, Amen.

3

Everything Comes From God

1 Chronicles 29:12 NKJV — Both riches and honor come from You, And You reign over all. In Your hand is power and might; In Your hand it is to make great And to give strength to all.

What can we give to Jehovah? Can we give Him our earnings? Does He want our houses or vehicles? Does He need us to provide food for Him to eat? What can we offer to Jehovah?

The cattle that roam the earth are His (Psalm 50:10).

The richest ores found in the depths of the earth belong to Him (Genesis 2:11-12.

He created the heavens and the earth (Genesis 1:1).

God formed and knitted our bodies in our mother's womb (Psalm 139:13).

The breath in our lungs comes from God (Acts 17:25).

What does Jehovah need from us?

Nothing.

This answer became apparent to David as he prepared to build the Temple. David amassed huge amounts of gold, silver, bronze, iron, and wood. He collected enormous quantities of onyx, precious stones, costly jewels, and a variety of fine stone and marble (1 Chronicles 29:1-2).

He donated from his collection and invited Israel to do the same. They contributed an abundance until they had enough to build the Temple (1 Chronicles 29:3-9).

But David recognized something about God that we all need to accept:

> *1 Chronicles 29:11-12 NLT — Yours, O LORD, is the greatness, the power, the glory, the victory, and the majesty. Everything in the heavens and on earth is yours, O LORD, and this is your kingdom. We adore you as the one who is over all things.*
>
> *Wealth and honor come from you alone, for you rule over everything. Power and might are in your hand, and at your discretion, people are made great and given strength.*

God needs nothing from us because it all belongs to Him. He has graciously given us everything and made us stewards over His creations.

God allows us to partner with Him, hoping that we'll open our hearts and accept Him as Sovereign Lord.

What can we give to Jehovah?

Nothing.

But God invites us into a relationship with Him. He invites us to fellowship with Him and then rewards us with even more blessings.

Prayer

Jehovah Jireh,

You are great and worthy to be praised. Everything we have comes from You and we glorify Your name. Thanks for Your generosity. May I never forget that You are the giver of all good things. In Jesus' name, Amen.

4

God's Kingdom Rules Over All

Psalm 103:19 NKJV — The LORD has established His throne in heaven, And His kingdom rules over all.

Regardless of where you live, your country has rulers. It may be a monarch, prime minister, or president. It may be a duke, duchess, chairman, or supreme leader. You may also have opinions about their leadership styles and powerful reasons when you exercise your right to vote.

Here's the thing: every kingdom on Earth is subject to God, whether they acknowledge His existence.

In 2 Chronicles 20, we read that the armies of the Moabites, Ammonites, and some Meunites declared war on Jehoshaphat, king of Judah.

These armies outpowered Judah in resources and numbers. But Jehoshaphat knew something the leaders of the attacking nations didn't. He knew the Lord of Hosts.

2 Chronicles 20:6 NLT — He prayed, "O LORD, God of our ancestors, you alone are the God who is in heaven.

You are ruler of all the kingdoms of the earth. You are powerful and mighty; no one can stand against you!"

Judah's underwhelming army defeated their adversaries without lifting a finger. They went into battle singing praises and the Lord delivered them (2 Chronicles 20:21-24).

God may not always choose to move in such a mighty way against the kings of the Earth. But no ruler takes possession of a country unless God allows it.

We may not always understand His choice of rulers or why He allows certain people to rise to power. But God is always sovereign over our earthly leaders.

No kingdom rises to power except that God allows it. The prophecies in Daniel prove that.

God's kingdom is everlasting (Psalms 145:13). It always was and always will be. It is dominant over every kingdom that has existed or will exist.

God rules over everything and everyone—always and forever.

Prayer

Elohim Chayim,

You are ruler over all the kingdoms of the world. May Your will be done on Earth as it is in heaven, for we are subject to Your care. In Jesus' name, Amen.

5

God Chooses Who to Have Mercy On

Romans 9:15 NLT — For God said to Moses, "I will show mercy to anyone I choose, and I will show compassion to anyone I choose."

Mercy is an intrinsic attribute of God's nature. This is the reason God gave Adam and Eve the promise of salvation instead of the instant death they'd expected after the Fall.

It is why God has not destroyed humanity despite our repeated transgressions against Him.

Yet this phrase: "I will have mercy on whomever I choose." sounds selfish.

Does God choose to have mercy on some but not on others?

Yes. But it's not as simple as we're thinking. So, let's put it into context to get a better understanding.

The phrase first appeared in Exodus 33:19. Moses had asked God for confirmation that He would go with the Israelites to the Promised Land and for God to teach him more about Himself (Exodus 33:12-16).

God affirmed that He'd go with the Israelites and Moses asked to see God's glorious presence (Exodus 33:18).

God's response and actions reiterated His merciful nature. There's no way Moses could have seen God's glorious presence and lived (Exodus 33:20).

Yet God showed Him mercy by:

1. Allowing the conversation to continue as long as it did.
2. Granting Moses's request as best as possible, given the limitations of man's sinful nature.

Eventually, Moses would go to heaven and see God face-to-face, but that day had not come yet.

God's mercy to Moses is a reminder that no one is holy enough to stand in His presence without being consumed, but He allows it anyway.

Let's look at it another way. Imagine a man with tremendous power and authority in the land. He can condemn people to death or give them the freedom they desire.

How would that man act? How would he show mercy? We only need to read history or check out current affairs to realize that absolute power corrupts absolutely.

A powerful man, who is not subject to the Holy Spirit, becomes a danger to those around him.

Thank goodness God is not like us! God is good, merciful, and just. We don't deserve salvation or mercy, but God grants it anyway.

We don't deserve His love and there's nothing we can do to earn it, but God lavishes it on us, anyway.

God doesn't look at what we own or consider our ethnicity, age, gender, or anything. Each of us stands before Him on level ground and God pities us all.

Prayer

Jehovah Chesed,

You are a God of mercy. Thank You for Your mercy toward me. Thank You for Your faithfulness. I give You glory, Lord. In Jesus' name, Amen.

6

God Made Everything For a Purpose

Proverbs 16:4 ESV — The LORD has made everything for its purpose, even the wicked for the day of trouble.

Have you ever seen an invention and wondered, Why on earth was that made? Does a particular tool and its purpose puzzle you?

For years, scientists claimed the appendix had no purpose in the human body. I've never believed that. Just because we can't figure out why something exists doesn't mean it doesn't have a purpose.

This lesson applies to other areas of our lives. You may not understand why something or someone exists, but God has a purpose for everything.

Only the Creator can determine why something exists. To understand this concept, ponder a piece of art, music, literature, or an outfit.

Though you may not comprehend the purpose behind a design's existence, its creator does. God, as the sovereign over all creation, determines what He creates.

In Genesis 1 & 2, we read the story of Creation. God made the heavens and the Earth.

He made the seas and everything that exists in them. Every tree, plant, and animal was first conceptualized and then created by God.

Why do lions exist? Because God created them.

Why do fruits exist? Because God created them.

Why do you exist? Because God created you.

My friend, your existence is not a coincidence. God has a purpose and plan for your life—one He'll reveal to you at the right time. I encourage you to ask God what He wants you to do. He'll be happy to share His plans with you.

Prayer

Jehovah Yatsar,

You are the Creator of everything. I may not understand why You made something, but I will praise You for its existence. Thank You for making all things for a purpose. Please reveal to me the purpose for which You created me. In Jesus' name, Amen.

7

God Has Power Over Sickness and Death

Deuteronomy 32:39 NKJV — 'Now see that I, even I, am He, And there is no God besides Me; I kill and I make alive; I wound and I heal; Nor is there any who can deliver from My hand.

The temptation to worship idols is as old as the Earth. In heaven, Satan became jealous because he wanted the worship that belonged to God (Ezekiel 28:16-17).

The devil's argument was so persuasive that he seduced a third of the angels who lost their place in heaven.

Then the devil brought his show to Earth (Revelation 12:7-9). Through guile and deception, the enemy convinced Eve to believe him over Jehovah. He convinced the woman to choose him over God (Genesis 3).

Dictionary.com defines an idol as any person or thing regarded with blind admiration, adoration, or devotion.

Christians often say that anything that we elevate to the place of the one true God is an idol. We also agree that the Bible is God's Word, yet from Genesis to Revelation, we read stories about men and women worshiping idols and images.

We read repeated accounts of God's people prostrating them-selves before idols.

Throughout the centuries, people have ascribed power to various gods, trusting them to control the elements in favor of those who worship them.

The result is always the same. There is no god like Jehovah.

No idol can control the times and seasons. No idol wields power over life, health, and death.

Only Jehovah can control the times and the seasons. Only He holds the power over life, death, and the grave.

After His people turned their backs on Him and worshiped idols, this is what God said about Himself:

> *Deuteronomy 32:39 NLT — Look now; I myself am he! There is no other god but me! I am the one who kills and gives life; I am the one who wounds and heals; no one can be rescued from my powerful hand!*

When Jesus came to Earth, He was the manifestation of these things. Jesus healed the sick and resurrected the dead. He conquered death and rose on the third day after His crucifixion. When He returns, no one will escape from His powerful hand.

Elohim is sovereign over all things, including sickness and death.

Prayer

Jehovah Rapha,

You are above death, hell, and the grave. Thank You for this reminder that only You deserve my praise. I glorify Your name because You're worthy to receive honor and glory. I praise You with every breath. In Jesus' name, Amen.

II

Why Is God Sovereign?

We have established God's sovereignty over heaven, Earth, and everything in it. But why is God dominant over all things? Why is He the One with ultimate control over everything and everyone?

8

What God Says Comes to Pass

Isaiah 55:11 NKJV — So shall My word be that goes forth from My mouth; It shall not return to Me void, But it shall accomplish what I please, And it shall prosper in the thing for which I sent it.

The Bible is full of accounts about God's creative power. The Lord speaks and His words come to pass. In Isaiah 55, God compared His Word to water affecting the growth of plants.

> *Isaiah 55:10 NLT — "The rain and snow come down from the heavens and stay on the ground to water the earth. They cause the grain to grow, producing seed for the farmer and bread for the hungry."*

God speaks, and it happens. Like our Creator, our words have power. Many people's lives changed forever because of what someone said to or about them. As Proverbs 18:21 says, 'Death and life are in the power of the tongue.'

The words we and others speak over our lives can have a long-reaching impact. But the words that God says supersedes all. What God says will happen because He has the creative power to make His words come to life. Let's look at a few of the things the Lord said.

> *Isaiah 9:6 NKJV — For unto us a Child is born, Unto us a Son is given; And the government will be upon His shoulder. And His name will be called Wonderful, Counselor, Mighty God, Everlasting Father, Prince of Peace.*

> *Isaiah 44:28 KJV — That saith of Cyrus, He is my shepherd, and shall perform all my pleasure: even saying to Jerusalem, Thou shalt be built; and to the temple, Thy foundation shall be laid.*

> *Jeremiah 29:10 NKJV — For thus says the LORD: After seventy years are completed at Babylon, I will visit you and perform My good word toward you, and cause you to return to this place.*

If God said it, we can believe it because all His promises are yes and Amen (2 Corinthians 1:20). If they haven't come true yet, they will.

Only a Sovereign Lord can ensure that every word He speaks is fulfilled.

Prayer

Jehovah Shammah,

Your Word is powerful and whatever You say will come true. I'm grateful that Your thoughts toward me are good. May You accomplish Your prophecies in the proper time. In Jesus' name, Amen.

9

God Created All Things

Colossians 1:16 NKJV — For by Him all things were created that are in heaven and that are on earth, visible and invisible, whether thrones or dominions or principalities or powers. All things were created through Him and for Him.

The first words of Genesis 1 are: "In the beginning, God created the heavens and the earth."

This simple statement encapsulates the universe and every life form that exists. It speaks to an intimate knowledge of things that humans, with all our technology, are still trying to comprehend.

If you study the story of Creation, you'll recognize that a logical and creative mind existed behind the design.

God created light and separated it from darkness (Genesis 1:2-5).

God collected matter, separated the heavens from the earth, and distinguished between them (Genesis 1:6-10).

He created vegetation. God gave each type the ability to reproduce itself (Genesis 1:11-12).

God created additional lights. Each had a purpose, a function, and a time to appear (Genesis 1:14-18).

He created animals, birds, and sea creatures. Each species can replicate itself (Genesis 1:20-22, 24-25).

Finally, God created a man and a woman. He gave them dominion over the Earth and reproductive ability (Genesis 1:26-28).

God did not create humankind until there was food for him to eat. He did not make food until the ecosystem to sustain it existed. God planned everything and executed His vision with perfection.

Some will offer alternative explanations for why the world and everything in it exists, but I believe what the Bible says.

> *Colossians 1:15-16 NLT — Christ is the visible image of the invisible God. He existed before anything was created and is supreme over all creation,*
>
> *for through him God created everything in the heavenly realms and on earth. He made the things we can see and the things we can't see—such as thrones, kingdoms, rulers, and authorities in the unseen world. Everything was created through him and for him.*

It is for this reason that God is Sovereign: He is Self-Existent. And because He is, He created the universe for His purposes. Let us give God the glory and honor He deserves.

Prayer

Elohim,

You are the Creator. You made this universe out of nothing and for Your purposes. Please work through me to accomplish Your will. In Jesus' name, Amen.

10

God Knows the Future

Isaiah 46:10 NLT — Only I can tell you the future before it even happens. Everything I plan will come to pass, for I do whatever I wish.

The future fascinates human beings. Our literature proves that. I remember being enthralled by *The Jetsons* as a child and thought flying cars would be the norm by the time I became an adult.

Even now we have movies and books set in the future. Analysts make predictions based on trends. People visit fortune tellers hoping to get a glimpse of what lies ahead.

Sometimes, people guess things right. But mostly, they're incorrect because only God knows the future. He can tell the end from the beginning.

Bible scholars have studied the prophecies in Daniel for ages and confirmed events God spoke about hundreds of years before they happened.

Scholars hope that if they can unlock the key, they can understand what the unfulfilled portions of the prophecies mean.

While Jesus was on Earth, He told the disciples many things that would happen before they did.

He told them about His betrayal, crucifixion, and resurrection (John 13:21, Matthew 16:21). Jesus told them about His ascension to heaven (John 14:1-3). Jesus promised to send them the Holy Spirit who would be their Comforter after He returned to heaven (John 14:16-17).

Christ prophesied about the destruction of the Temple and Jerusalem (Matthew 24:1-2). Some disciples lived to see many of Jesus' predictions come true. What a faith-building experience that must have been!

Modern believers read about the prophecies of God and look forward to the ones that haven't occurred yet. We know they will come true because of the promises and prophecies already fulfilled.

Who can predict the future but the One who has control over it?

God knows the future and encourages us to trust Him with our lives and leave the future in His hands.

Prayer

El Roi,

I come to You because You know the future. You are the God who knows the end from the beginning. I commit my life to You. Use me, Lord, for Your purposes. In Jesus' name, Amen.

11

God Can Do Impossible Things

Luke 18:27 NIV — Jesus replied, "What is impossible with man is possible with God."

The rich young ruler went to Jesus and asked a question that many wanted to know the answer to: "Good Teacher, what shall I do to inherit eternal life?" (Luke 18:18 NKJV)

Jesus told him to keep the commandments and listed five out of the ten (Luke 18:20). The ruler was confident that he'd kept the Law since his youth. Jesus challenged him to sell everything and give it to the poor (Luke 18:21-23).

This was a deal-breaker because he was wealthy. Jesus marveled at the impossibility of a rich man making it into heaven (Luke 18:24-26).

The people were amazed. If the wealthy didn't have what it takes to make it into heaven, who did?

Matthew 19:26 NLT — Jesus looked at them intently and said, "Humanly speaking, it is impossible. But with God everything is possible."

The word translated as impossible is adýnatos[1] (pronounced ad-oo'-nat-os). Adýnatos means unable, i.e. weak (literally or figuratively).

Adýnatos also means impossible, could not do, impotent, and not possible.

The word translated as possible is dynatós[2] (pronounced doo-nat-os'). Dynatós means powerful or capable (literally or figuratively).

Dynatós means able, mighty, possible, power, and strong.

Man is adýnatos, but God is dynatós. Man is weak, but God is strong. The things a man cannot conceive, much less action, are trivial matters for God.

Salvation was not something man could accomplish on his own. He needed a Savior—a sinless Person to suffer the trial of humanity without sin.

This is not the only impossible thing that God has done. God opens the womb of the barren. He restores sight to the blind, and hearing to the deaf. God heals the sick and resurrects the dead.

As the prophet Jeremiah said:

> *"Ah, Sovereign LORD, you have made the heavens and the earth by your great power and outstretched arm. Nothing is too hard for you" (Jeremiah 32:17 NIV).*

---

[1] "G102 - adynatos - Strong's Greek Lexicon (KJV)." Blue Letter Bible. Web. 5 Apr, 2024.

[2] "G1415 - dynatos - Strong's Greek Lexicon (KJV)." Blue Letter Bible. Web. 5 Apr, 2024.

God does impossible things because He is Sovereign over every-thing.

Prayer

El Shaddai,

You are the only one who can save. Please rescue me from the evil one. Into Your hands, I commend my spirit. In Jesus' name, Amen.

12

God Will Judge Everyone

*Romans 14:11 NIV — It is written: " 'As surely as I live,' says the
Lord, 'every knee will bow before me; every tongue will
acknowledge God.' "*

When an individual breaks the laws of a country, he must face the consequences. Depending on his crimes, there may be a judiciary hearing where the individual receives a verdict and a sentence.

He may stand before a judge, while a lawyer argues his case. Or a jury may review his case and return a judgment. In either case, a judge presides over the proceedings and can issue a verdict.

Regardless of how carefully they examine the arguments and evidence, or how much experience the legal team or judge has, they will make mistakes.

Innocent people get convicted, sent to jail, and even executed. Guilty people get exonerated and some continue to commit their crimes.

Where is the justice?

In a flawed world, we do our best to protect the rights of each

36

individual and uphold law and order. It's not a perfect system. But there will come a time when God will be our Judge.

> *Romans 14:10-12 NIV — You, then, why do you judge your brother or sister? Or why do you treat them with contempt? For we will all stand before God's judgment seat.*
>
> *It is written: " 'As surely as I live,' says the Lord, 'every knee will bow before me; every tongue will acknowledge God.' "*

Each of us will account for ourselves to God. The Lord is omnipresent and omniscient. He is present everywhere and with everyone. When He judges us, He won't make a mistake. He knows everything we've done—He even knows our hearts.

The Lord loves justice. He vindicates the innocent and punishes the guilty. He has the right to do that because He's our Sovereign Lord.

Earthly judges accept bribes or are misled by their emotions or intellect. The Lord is infallible. He is incorruptible. His judgment will stand.

Prayer

Jehovah Shâphaṭ,

You alone can judge because You see and know all things. Vindicate the innocent, Lord, and punish the wicked, for I ask it in Jesus' name. Amen.

13

God Empowers Us

Isaiah 64:8 NLT — And yet, O LORD, you are our Father. We are the clay, and you are the potter. We all are formed by your hand.

Where does the energy to work come from? How are ideas generated? Where do we get our abilities from?

Everything originates from God. He created us and gave us all the resources. He also gave us free will to choose how to use the gifts He has blessed us with.

God gives to the just and the unjust. Sadly, people misuse resources, talents, and gifts, sometimes in ways harmful to others.

When we accept the Lord as Sovereign, God uses us to accomplish marvelous things.

Ephesians 2:10 KJV — For we are his workmanship, created in Christ Jesus unto good works, which God hath before ordained that we should walk in them.

The word translated as ordained is proetoimázō (pronounced pro-et-oy-mad'-zo). Proetoimázō means to fit up in advance (literally or figuratively) or prepare afore.

We can only do things because God, through the power of the Holy Spirit, does them through us.

We are empowered to do things because Christ lives in us and works through us.

But what about the person who doesn't believe in God? How does Christ empower them?

It is God who gives us the breath of life. He empowers our brains to work and our limbs to move. God gives us the gift of language and communication.

Take away the things the Lord has given to man and you have nothing. As the psalmist puts it:

> *Psalm 103:14 NLT — For he knows how weak we are; he remembers we are only dust.*

Without God, we are nothing and can do nothing. He is the Sovereign Lord and we are the creatures of His hand.

Prayer

Adonai Elohim,

Have mercy on me, Your creation. Empower me to do the work for which I was created so I may glorify Your name. In Jesus' name, Amen.

14

Even the Animals Are Subject to God

Matthew 10:29 NKJV — "Are not two sparrows sold for a copper coin? And not one of them falls to the ground apart from your Father's will."

Imagine a world where hunters caught animals in their traps, but the creatures survived. A world where we slaughter animals, but they don't die.

No, it's not a strange dystopian world. I use this illustration to highlight that even the animals belong to God. Not a single one of them dies without Him allowing it.

When God created the world, He gave mankind dominion over the animals (Genesis 1:26). However, He didn't designate animals as food, so we can assume that the animals were more companions and friends than prey.

This changed after The Great Flood. Animals could be eaten, and their relationship with mankind changed.

Genesis 9:2 NLT — All the animals of the earth, all the birds of the sky, all the small animals that scurry along

the ground, and all the fish in the sea will look on you
with fear and terror. I have placed them in your power.

In both cases, God set up the hierarchy. You can't give away what doesn't belong to you (at least, you shouldn't!).

The animals belong to God and respond to His commands, sometimes better than humans. We see a vivid depiction of that in Numbers 22.

The Lord told Balaam not to go with King Balak's messengers. However, because it was profitable for Balaam, he disobeyed God and went.

Balaam's donkey tried to turn back three times because it saw the angel of the Lord. Balaam beat the donkey for refusing to follow the path, then the animal spoke to him.

Who but God could make a donkey speak?

This is not the only story where God exercised His dominance over the animals. He sent frogs, locusts, and flies to show His power in Egypt.

God sent a whale to swallow Jonah and then deposit him on land (Jonah 1:17, 2:10). He sent ravens to feed Elijah (1 Kings 17:3-4).

He sent a pack of bears to defend Elisha (2 Kings 23-25). God shut the mouths of lions (Daniel 6:22).

Jehovah is the Sovereign Lord because He commands every-thing in the universe. We would do well to obey Him.

Prayer

El Elyon,

Even the animals obey You. Help me be more obedient to Your will. In Jesus' name, Amen.

III

Responding to God's Sovereignty

We've explored what God's sovereignty means and why He's sovereign. Let's consider how we should respond to God's sovereignty.

15

Recognize That Our Time Is In God's Hands

James 4:15 NKJV — Instead you ought to say, "If the Lord wills, we shall live and do this or that."

Do you enjoy making plans? Do you know what you'll be doing a week from now? How about this time next year?

While it is good for us to have plans and desires for our lives, they should always be flexible.

In Luke 12:13-21, Jesus told the parable of the rich fool. The man's fields had yielded an abundant harvest, and his first instinct was to build a bigger barn and store his excess.

While this parable is a lesson against greed and selfishness, it also reminds us to use our time wisely.

The rich man anticipated a life of ease—one where he could enjoy the harvest without working. He didn't know that his time on earth was short.

My friend, we don't know when our lives will end. We can make five-year plans not knowing we only have two years left.

Do I say this to discourage you? No. I encourage you to dream about the future and make plans with God. Recognize that time is a privilege—a gift from our heavenly Father.

This was the advice given in James 4:13-15.

> *James 4:13-15 NIV — Now listen, you who say, "Today or tomorrow we will go to this or that city, spend a year there, carry on business and make money."*
>
> *Why, you do not even know what will happen tomorrow. What is your life? You are a mist that appears for a little while and then vanishes.*
>
> *Instead, you ought to say, "If it is the Lord's will, we will live and do this or that."*

Make plans, but remember that it is God who determines whether we'll be able to accomplish them or not.

Submit your plans into God's hands, trusting Him to help you achieve them or to replace them with better ones.

Prayer

Abba,

You are Alpha and Omega, the beginning and the end. You are outside of time because You created it. Help me make plans with You and to trust You with the results. In Jesus' name, Amen.

16

Obey Those in Authority

Romans 13:1 NKJV — Let every soul be subject to the governing authorities. For there is no authority except from God, and the authorities that exist are appointed by God.

Depending on where you live, elections can be polarizing. Residents square off against each other as they argue the merits of the platforms of the men and women running for office.

Once the ballots are counted, people disagree with the results. Persons may claim someone rigged the elections or demand a recount.

This uncertainty can continue for weeks, sometimes months, after the elections. People forget that even if they disagree with the elected officials, all power comes from God.

This statement may lead you to research countries governed by despots as proof that this couldn't be true. I hear you. When we see how people abuse power, we wonder if there's been a mistake.

Let us remember that it is God's purpose that will prevail. We don't understand why He allows elected officials to hold office, but we can trust that God has a plan.

According to Romans 13:1-7, this is how we should respond to governing officials:

1. Submit to their authority (Romans 13:1).
2. Do not rebel against the authorities lest we be punished (Romans 13:2).
3. Do what is right and obey the law (Romans 13:3).
4. Pay your taxes and government fees (Romans 13:6-7).
5. Respect and honor those in authority (Romans 13:7).

Government officials are not the only people we should submit to.

1. God wants children to obey and honor their parents (Ephesians 6:1-3).
2. Parents are to treat children in a way that honors God (Ephesians 6:4).
3. Servants are to obey and serve their masters (Ephesians 6:5-8).
4. Masters are to honor their servants out of respect for God (Ephesians 6:9).
5. There should be mutual submission between husbands and wives. For wives, that means respecting their husband's authority. For husbands, that means loving their wives with the same sacrificial love God has for the church (Ephesians 5:21-33.
6. Members of the church should respect their spiritual leaders (Hebrews 13:7).
7. Young people should submit to the authority of their elders

(1 Peter 5:5).

Goodness! Do you see how important obedience is to God?

We honor God's sovereignty over our lives when we respect those in authority over us.

Prayer

El Gibbor,

I submit to Your authority. Please help me respect my earthly rulers and others in authority. I may not always agree with their actions, but You have a plan and I trust You.

May Your will be done on Earth as it is in heaven. In Jesus' name, Amen.

17

Remember God Uses Even Evil Things For Good

Romans 8:28 NLT — And we know that God causes everything to work together for the good of those who love God and are called according to his purpose for them.

Wouldn't it be wonderful if we lived in a world where only good things happened? Sadly, because of sin, bad things happen in a day, often multiple times. The beautiful thing is that God redeems even on our worst days, and the events we wished had never happened.

We saw this play out in Joseph's life. As the firstborn of Rachel, Jacob's favorite wife, his life was privileged. Joseph was his father's favorite son and Jacob didn't care who knew it.

This made Joseph's brothers angry until they sold him into slavery. Being a slave would have been a strange experience for Joseph.

He was subject to his masters and had to do their bidding. He was in a new country, surrounded by strange gods. Joseph may have had to learn the language to survive in an unfamiliar country.

Eventually, Potiphar appointed Joseph as his attendant and put him in charge of his entire household (Genesis 39:4). For a slave, things don't get better than this.

But it didn't last. Joseph was imprisoned. Again, Joseph had to learn the expectations of his new position. But the Lord elevated him over the other prisoners (Genesis 39:22).

I'm sure these three environments differed from each other. In Potiphar's house and the prison, Joseph had responsibility and a semblance of power, but he wasn't free. He had to obey those set above him.

Fast-forward to Pharaoh's dream and a long-forgotten promise and Joseph was released from prison and elevated to the position of second in command to Pharaoh (Genesis 41:40-41).

Things were looking up for Joseph. He had power, freedom, a wife, and children, but was still living in a different country from his family. Joseph wouldn't see his family until the famine.

Joseph's brothers later expressed their regrets for selling him into slavery. Their actions had haunted them for years, and even though Joseph forgave them, they still felt guilty (Genesis 50:17-18). Joseph realized something his brothers hadn't:

> *Genesis 50:20 NKJV — "But as for you, you meant evil against me; but God meant it for good, in order to bring it about as it is this day, to save many people alive."*

If Joseph hadn't been a slave, he wouldn't have run amok of Potiphar's wife and imprisoned.

If Joseph hadn't been in prison, he wouldn't have met Pharaoh's chief cup-bearer and chief baker. He wouldn't have interpreted their dreams.

Joseph wouldn't have been there to decipher the Pharaoh's disturbing dreams. He wouldn't have been in the position to rescue his family and prevent them from dying in the famine.

My friend, God used the events in Joseph's life to accomplish His marvelous plan. Jehovah is omnipresent and omniscient. He sees the end from the beginning. God can transform your worst experiences into blessings.

My friend, submit to God and believe He has excellent plans for your life.

Prayer

Jehovah Rohi,

You are in control, God. You see everything and know everything. I trust You to work out the plans You have for my life. In Jesus' name, Amen.

18

Be Holy and Blameless Before God

Ephesians 1:4 NLT — Even before he made the world, God loved us and chose us in Christ to be holy and without fault in his eyes.

One of God's intrinsic characteristics is holiness.

The Merriam-Webster Dictionary defines holy as exalted or worthy of complete devotion as one perfect in goodness and righteousness.

God is worthy of our complete devotion because of who He is. Because God is holy, He wants His people to be holy (Leviticus 19:2).

When He chose Israel as His special people, He called them a "kingdom of priests", His holy nation (Exodus 19:6).

Why is our holiness so important to God?

When God created Adam and Eve, they were perfect. Before they sinned, God communed with them face-to-face (Genesis 3:8).

After the Fall this was no longer possible because sinful people cannot come into the presence of a holy God and live (Exodus 33:20).

Because God desires a relationship with us, He made a way to commune with us through His Son, Jesus.

Jesus is our righteousness. When we accept Christ as our Lord and Savior, He ascribes His righteousness to us (2 Corinthians 5:21). This allows us to come into the presence of God and not die.

Even though we have sinned, God bestowed His holiness on us.

> *Ephesians 1:3–4 NLT — All praise to God, the Father of our Lord Jesus Christ, who has blessed us with every spiritual blessing in the heavenly realms because we are united with Christ.*
>
> *Even before he made the world, God loved us and chose us in Christ to be holy and without fault in his eyes.*

Holiness is a privilege and a gift. One that God grants us because He chooses to.

God calls His people to holiness because He's a holy God. After all that God has done for us, He asks us to hold ourselves to a higher standard than the world.

Prayer

Jehovah Tsidkenu,

Thank You for the privilege of a communal relationship. Please make me holy as You are holy, Lord. In Jesus' name, Amen.

19

Submit Everything Into God's Hands

Proverbs 3:5-6 NKJV — Trust in the LORD with all your heart, And lean not on your own understanding; In all your ways acknowledge Him, And He shall direct your paths.

Autonomy is something we strive for. We want to be in control of our lives and our destinies. This is because too often we've experienced or witnessed atrocities done to people whose lives were under the control of the wrong people.

I suspect this fear of being abused or taken advantage of lies behind our desire for control. It may be the reason we struggle to submit to God.

But here's the thing: God is infinitely good. His mercy is never ending and His love is everlasting. We don't have to worry that He'll take advantage of us or run roughshod over our rights.

When we accept God's sovereignty, we submit everything into His hands.

What does submission look like?

It means we release our lives into His care. We give Him our talents and our time. We release our spouses, children, and family into God's control.

Proverbs 3:5-6 gives us a three-step process for this.

1. **Trust God with your entire heart and everything you are.**

The word translated as trust is bâṭach[3] (pronounced baw-takh'). Bâṭach means to hie for refuge, to trust, or be confident.

Trusting God means believing He'll do what's best for us, even if it doesn't turn out how we hoped.

2. **Don't rely on your understanding.**

The word translated as "your own understanding[4]" is bîynâh (pronounced bee-naw'). Bîynâh means understanding, knowledge, or wisdom.

Our knowledge is finite. We don't have complete information about anything. It, therefore, means that our interpretation will be flawed. God has perfect knowledge and wisdom. Rather than rely on ourselves, let's depend on God.

3. **Acknowledge God in every area of your life.**

Recognize that God is concerned with everything you do and submit each area of your life to Him. Remember that God is Sovereign. Surrender control to Him.

---

[3] "H982 - bāṭaḥ - Strong's Hebrew Lexicon (KJV)." Blue Letter Bible. Web. 5 Apr, 2024.

[4] "H998 - bînâ - Strong's Hebrew Lexicon (KJV)." Blue Letter Bible. Web. 5 Apr, 2024.

When you do these three things, the Lord will direct your path.

The word translated as direct is yâshar[5] (pronounced yaw-shar'). Yâshar means to be straight or even. Figuratively, yâshar means to be or make right, pleasant, or prosperous.

God is trustworthy. Surrender your life to Him, and He will smooth the path before you.

Prayer

El Olam,

I surrender all—my desires, dreams, gifts, and talents. I surrender my family, friends, and everything I have into Your hands. Direct my path, Lord. I trust You. In Jesus' name, Amen.

---

[5] "H3474 - yāšar - Strong's Hebrew Lexicon (KJV)." Blue Letter Bible. Web. 5 Apr, 2024.

20

Don't Question the Creator

Romans 9:20 NKJV — But indeed, O man, who are you to reply against God? Will the thing formed say to him who formed it, "Why have you made me like this?"

Do you love the reflection that greets you in the mirror? Do you celebrate the gifts and talents God has given you?

Maybe you wish you were more like someone else. Or you don't understand how God can use you the way you are.

We live in a world where we can get a front-row seat into other people's lives, and have more people than ever to compare ourselves to.

There's always someone who is further along the road you're traveling. Sometimes, it causes us to falter in our purpose and question God.

Why didn't You make me a different way—more like her?

Why didn't You give me that talent instead of the one I have?

Why can't my family act more like hers?

These questions can go on until they create a nature of

ingratitude. We lose sight of what God has blessed us with because we're too busy wishing for what somebody else has.

In Romans 9, the apostle Paul talks about the selection of Israel. God hadn't chosen the Israelites because they'd done anything magnificent. He chose them for His own reasons and purposes—neither of which He has to explain to anyone.

Similarly, God chooses to whom He'll offer mercy (Romans 9:15-26). We may disagree with God's choices or dislike His methodology, but as Paul puts it:

> *Romans 9:20 NIV — But who are you, a human being, to talk back to God? "Shall what is formed say to the one who formed it, 'Why did you make me like this?'"*

God decides on the gifts and talents He bestows to each person. He decides how they're made and for what purpose.

The Creator honors us by giving us the freedom to choose. That freedom doesn't give us the right to question His Sovereign decisions.

Let me put it another way. You may disagree with the decisions made by the leaders of your country. But you're not storming into their homes or parliament to make your displeasure known, are you? (At least, I hope not!)

No, we obey the laws of our country just as we obey God's Laws. Do not argue with your Creator, instead, partner with Him to fulfill His purpose for your life.

Prayer

El Eloah,

Forgive me for every time I've questioned how I was made, my gifts and talents, or the purpose for which You created me. Help me celebrate and walk in my purpose. In Jesus' name, Amen.

21

Worship and Honor the Lord

Revelation 4:11 NKJV — "You are worthy, O Lord, To receive glory and honor and power; For You created all things, And by Your will they exist and were created."

In Revelation 4, we're given a glimpse into God's throne room. The throne room is the seat of power. Decisions are made in a throne room. Dignitaries pay tribute to monarchs in this room.

It shouldn't surprise us that worship occurs in God's throne room.

Revelation 4:8 NLT — Each of these living beings had six wings, and their wings were covered all over with eyes, inside and out. Day after day and night after night they keep on saying, "Holy, holy, holy is the Lord God, the Almighty— the one who always was, who is, and who is still to come."

The angels who sit in the presence of God worship the Creator because of His sovereignty. They acknowledge His holiness and omnipresence.

If the angels who didn't sin or transgress God's Law bow down to worship Him, how much more should we?

The Bible says we're conceived in sin and shaped in iniquity (Psalm 51:5). Our very existence is offensive to God. It is only because of His mercy that we exist.

God's love for humanity inspired Him to design a way for us not to be destroyed. Why shouldn't we worship Him?

Our worship should first flow out of gratitude because He created us. It should gush out of our spirits because He redeemed us. Praise should burst out of our mouths because God sustains us.

My friend, without God, we would not exist. Without God, we cannot survive. Everything we have exists because God created it. Everything we have is because God allows us to have them.

Worship the Lord with every fiber of your being. Praise the Lord who is faithful even when you are not.

All praises to the King of kings and Lord of lords. Praise Him from whom all blessings flow. Let everything that has breath praise the Lord!

Prayer

Immanuel,

All praises go to You because only You deserve the glory, honor, and praise. I am honored that You have mercy on me. I give you glory, Lord. In Jesus' name, Amen.

IV

Additional Resources

22

3 Profound Reasons Idolatry Is a Sin

The second commandment warns us against idolatry, but have you ever wondered what is idolatry or some things that can become idols?

Maybe you think idolatry ended with the Israelites and don't see how it applies to believers today. Let's study this topic and see how we can avoid the pitfalls.

What is Idolatry?

The Oxford Dictionary Online defines idolatry as extreme admiration, love, or reverence for something or someone.

While this gives us a starting point, let's go deeper.

The International Standard Bible Encyclopedia defines idolatry[6] in the following ways:

---

[6] Orr, James, M.A., D.D. General Editor. "Entry for 'IDOLATRY'". "International Standard Bible Encyclopedia". 1915.

- the worship of idols, or the worship of false gods by means of idols,
- any worship of false gods, whether by images or otherwise,
- the worship of Yahweh through visible symbols giving to any creature or human creation the honor or devotion which belonged to God alone, the giving to any human desire precedence over God's will.

Whew! That's quite a mouthful, so let's break it down. Idolatry is:

- Anything we worship (express adoration or reverence to) that is not the Creator is idolatry.
- If we create an image and claim that it is the Creator and worship it, it becomes idolatry.
- Any deity we worship that is not the Creator is an idol.
- If we give anyone the honor that belongs to the Creator or put a human desire ahead of God's will, it's an idol.

What things can be idols?

Anything elevated to the place that belongs to Jehovah becomes an idol. So what are some things that can become idols? When we read the Bible, we see the children of Israel worshiping images or the deities of foreign nations.

They put their faith in these items that were inanimate and useless. Could a god that man created rescue, heal, or deliver?

The answer seems obvious today, yet this was a trap the

---

https://www.biblestudytools.com/encyclopedias/isbe/idolatry.html

Israelites fell into repeatedly. But maybe we shouldn't be pointing fingers at the children of Israel. After all, we have idols of our own today. Because the trouble with idolatry is that anything can become an idol.

> *Some trust in chariots and some in horses, but we trust in the name of the LORD our God.*
> *Psalm 20:7 NIV*

Let's rewrite this verse using modern-day items.

Some trust in money and some in fame. Some trust in their family or their friends. Others trust in their parents or their children. Some trust in people and others in themselves.

Is it becoming clearer? My friend, idolatry is a slippery slope we can slide down many times. The trick is not to stay down or to keep sliding once we identify our idols.

Why Is Idolatry a Sin?

The simple answer is that it breaks the Lord's commandment. Now you may ask which commandment and most persons will say the second. I agree with that answer but would like to expand on it.

Let's look at the first three commandments in Exodus 20.

> *And God spoke all these words, saying:*
> *"I am the Lord your God, who brought you out of the*

land of Egypt, out of the house of bondage.

"You shall have no other gods before Me.

"You shall not make for yourself a carved image—any likeness of anything that is in heaven above, or that is in the earth beneath, or that is in the water under the earth; you shall not bow down to them nor serve them. For I, the Lord your God, am a jealous God, visiting the iniquity of the fathers upon the children to the third and fourth generations of those who hate Me, but showing mercy to thousands, to those who love Me and keep My commandments.

"You shall not take the name of the Lord your God in vain, for the Lord will not hold him guiltless who takes His name in vain" (Exodus 20:1-7 NKJV).

Do you realize how fluid the first three commandments are? It's almost as if one gives rise to the next. If you're anything like me, you might find it difficult to separate them because they are so closely intertwined.

Let's explain why idolatry is a sin by studying an example in the Bible.

Shortly after the Lord gave the people the commandment, Moses ascended the mountain to speak with God. In his absence, the people became restless and demanded that Aaron make a god for them.

Aaron created a golden calf, and the Israelites worshipped the statue. You can read the full account in Exodus 32. Let's talk about how this act of idolatry obliterated multiple command-ments.

1. **When the Israelites worshiped the calf, they placed this god**

before their Creator. That broke the first commandment.

They even credited the golden calf with what God had done for them. Look at the Israelites' statement after Aaron made the calf:

> *Then they said, "This is your god, O Israel, that brought you out of the land of Egypt!" Exodus 32:4 NKJV*

This negated the statement God made at the beginning of the Ten Commandments:

> *"I am the Lord your God, who brought you out of the land of Egypt, out of the house of bondage." Exodus 20:2 NKJV*

2. When they created the calf, the Israelites broke the second commandment by making for themselves a carved image. Then they bowed down before it.

Now you may say, "I've read that account and there's no mention of them bowing down before the calf" and you'd be correct. Let's review Exodus 20:5 again.

> *Thou shalt not bow down thyself to them, nor serve them: for I the LORD thy God am a jealous God, visiting the iniquity of the fathers upon the children unto the third and fourth generation of them that hate me;– Exodus 20:5 KJV*

The word translated as "bow down thyself" is the Hebrew

word shâchâh[7], (pronounced shaw-khaw'). Shâchâh means to depress, i.e. prostrate (especially in homage to royalty or God). While it means to bow oneself down, it could also have been translated as worship.

When God said His people were not to bow down before idols, He meant they were not to worship them. And there was worship happening in the story of the golden calf. They even brought offerings to the calf (Exodus 32:6-8).

3. The third commandment says we should "not take the name of the Lord your God in vain" (Exodus 20:7).

The word translated as vain was the Hebrew word shâv[e'8], (pronounced shawv) and could also have been translated to mean false(-ly), lie, or lying. Shâv[e'] is used in the Bible to mean emptiness, nothingness, or vanity.

When they ascribed the Lord's name to the golden calf (Exodus 32:5), they took the name of the Lord in vain. In one act, they broke three commandments (and there may have been more). Do you see now why idolatry is a sin?

Idolatry is a deceptive act that puts someone or something else in a place that only Jehovah can occupy.

---

7 "H7812 - šāḥâ - Strong's Hebrew Lexicon (KJV)." Blue Letter Bible. Web. 5 Apr, 2024.

8 "H7723 - šāv' - Strong's Hebrew Lexicon (KJV)." Blue Letter Bible. Web. 5 Apr, 2024.

Modern-day Idolatry

We may not create a golden image and bow down before it, but modern-day idolatry is something many of us struggle with. We put our families, jobs, possessions, and even worries and fears in the center of our hearts and lives.

My friend, it should not be so. God has done too many things for us, including sending Christ to die for our sins. Let us discard our modern-day idols and revere Jehovah as our Sovereign and King.

What idols do you have in your life? Even more important, what steps will you take to topple those idols[9]?

---

[9] This chapter was originally published as What is Idolatry? 3 Profound Reasons Idolatry is a Sin, March 2, 2023, https://hebrews12endurance.com/**what-is-idolatry.** The chapter was updated and modified for this book.

23

4 Simple Steps to Grow in Godliness

As believers, growing in godliness is a major pursuit. We want to learn to be more like God. We want our lives to reflect His character so we can point others to Him. But what does it mean to be godly?

What is the Biblical Meaning of Godliness?

Paul's first letter to Timothy spoke about what it meant to be godly. The word godly or godliness occurs 11 times in First Timothy.

The word translated as godliness in Timothy is the Greek word eusébeia[10], (pronounced yoo-seb'-i-ah). It could have been translated to mean piety; specially, the gospel scheme, godliness, or holiness.

---

[10] "G2150 – eusebeia – Strong's Greek Lexicon (KJV)." Blue Letter Bible. Web. 5 Apr, 2024.

Another word for godliness is piety, which means reverence towards God, and the things associated with Him.

According to the Oxford Dictionary, godliness is the quality of being devoutly religious or piety. But being godly is more than an act of being religious. It goes beyond our actions and reflects the state of our hearts and posture before God.

The root word for eusébeia is eusebés[11], (pronounced yoo-seb-ace'); meaning well-reverent, i.e. pious, devout, godly. This brings us full circle to our English definition. A godly person follows God's laws and shows Him the proper reverence.

What does it mean to be godly?

Let me explain what "godliness concerns our posture before God" means. I'm sure you know at least one person who professes to be a believer.

They do all the "right" things, but they don't seem to reflect the love Christ said would be the identifying mark of His disciples. Sadly, they possess all the trappings of Christianity, having none of the heart.

A godly person aspires to be like God. To tell you who God is would take more words than exist in the universe, but we can begin by saying that God is good. He is the originator and giver of every good thing.

God is love (1 John 4:8). He is the originator and epitome of

---

[11] "G2152 - eusebēs - Strong's Greek Lexicon (KJV)." Blue Letter Bible. Web. 5 Apr, 2024.

love.

The Bible tells us about God. The person who wants to grow in godliness should become a student of the Word. Thankfully, we have an example in Christ. If you want to know what godliness is (and what it isn't) look at Jesus.

Importance of Godliness

But why is godliness important? The Bible tells us to pursue godliness (1 Timothy 6:11 NIV). This tells me that godliness is not our natural state. How can it be when every intention of our heart is only evil continually and our hearts are desperately wicked?

We only have to examine a child for a few minutes to understand that sin is such an ingrained part of our nature that no one has to teach a child how to do wrong...it simply happens.

Yet sin separates us from God and calls for the death penalty, a price we cannot pay to repair our relationship with God. Thankfully, we don't have to because God sent His Son as the perfect sacrifice for our imperfect lives.

Godliness is necessary for reconciliation with God. If we want to receive the reward for being faithful, we put off our old character and take on the righteousness of God. Are you beginning to see the importance of having a godly character?

What Does the Bible Say About Godliness?

The Bible gives us many teachings on the importance of godliness and the resources to accomplish it. Here are a few scriptural references:

For while bodily training is of some value, godliness is of value in every way, as it holds promise for the present life and also for the life to come (1 Timothy 4:8 ESV).

In fact, everyone who wants to live a godly life in Christ Jesus will be persecuted,
    while evildoers and impostors will go from bad to worse, deceiving and being deceived (2 Timothy 3:12–12 NIV).

He has shown you, O man, what is good; and what does the Lord require of you but to do justly, to love mercy, and to walk humbly with your God? (Micah 6:8 NKJV)

What is the Difference Between Holiness and Godliness?

You may wonder if there's a difference between godliness and holiness. There is, but the difference is so subtle as to make it difficult to define.

One of God's intrinsic qualities is His holiness. To be holy is to be set apart. It is to be sacred or designated for a specific purpose. As Christians, God instructed us to be holy because He is holy (Leviticus 19:2).

But holiness is a trait that we can't aspire to. We can reflect

God's holiness through communion with Christ, but it's not an intrinsic part of who we are.

Godliness is a trait we can possess. As we become more like God, we display what it means to be dedicated to pursuing the things of God.

How to Grow in Godliness

So how do we go about building a godly character? It starts with an acknowledgment that we are sinful and need a Savior. Next, we must pursue godliness. Psalm 1 gives us an outline of what it looks like to build a godly character.

1. Don't follow the advice or counsel of wicked or ungodly people (Psalm 1:1).
2. Don't associate or surround yourself with sinners and scoffers (Psalm 1:1).
3. Delight in God's law (Psalm 1:2).
4. Meditate on God's Word day and night (Psalm 1:2).

It seems easy, yet it hints at habits that must become a part of our daily lives if we are to grow in godliness. These habits include choosing our friends wisely, Bible study, and being careful about our watching and reading habits.

Characteristics of Godliness

Micah 6:8 epitomized the characteristics of godliness in a single verse. To be godly is to:

- *do what is just*
- *love mercy, and*
- *walk humbly with God*

There are many examples of godliness in the Bible, and they all exhibit the traits above. Just think about Abraham, Joshua, Joseph, Noah, Job, the apostles, Jesus...

They all sought to do the right things, following the laws of God and showing love to their fellow man.

Growing in godliness is a critical skill for every believer. I encourage you to spend some time thinking about how you can strengthen your relationship with God[12].

---

[12] this chapter was initially published as 4 Simple Steps to Grow in Godliness, June 12, 2021, https://hebrews12endurance.com/**how-to-grow-in-godliness**/. It was modified and updated for this book.

24

Names of God

This devotional included each of the names for God below. Below are the meanings so you can use them in your devotional time.

- Abba - Father
- Adonai - Lord, Master, Sovereign Master
- Adonai Elohim - My Great Lord
- El Eloah - The High God
- El Elyon - The Most High God
- El Gibbor - Mighty God
- El Olam - Everlasting God or Eternal God
- El Roi - The God Who Sees
- El Shaddai - God Almighty
- Elohim - Supreme God
- Elohim Chayim - The Living God
- Jehovah Jireh - The Lord Will Provide
- Jehovah Chesed - God of Forgiveness
- Jehovah Rapha - The God Who Heals
- Jehovah Rohi - God the Shepherd

- Jehovah Shammah – The Lord is there
- Jehovah Shâphaṭ – The Lord Our Judge
- Jehovah Tsidkenu – Lord Our Righteousness
- Jehovah Yatsar – God Our Potter
- Immanuel – God is With us
- Yahweh – The Self-Existent One

About Aminata

Aminata Coote's love affair with books began with an upside-down copy of Silas Marner. She's passionate about helping women understand the truth of the Bible for themselves.

She writes stories and books that point to a God bigger than our failings and provide hope to others. Aminata is also the author of several Bible studies and devotionals.

She lives in Montego Bay, Jamaica with her husband and son.

Connect with her on her website, aminatacoote.com, or on Instagram or Facebook @aminatacoote. Learn more about her books at https://aminatacoote.com/books-by-aminata-coote/
.

If you're a fan of Christian romance and would like to join my community, sign up for my newsletter at https://tinyurl.com/FreeReadingJournal. I'll send you a free reading journal.

Other Books by Aminata

Christian Living

Face Your Fear: Choose Faith Over Fear

Affirmations for Christian Women: Biblical Affirmations for Spiritual and Emotional Self-Care

7 Lessons on Endurance from Hebrews 12:1-2

Through God's Eyes: Marriage Lessons for Women

Unwavering: How to Stand Strong in Your Faith

Bible Study Workbooks

The Book of Haggai Bible Study Workbook

Bible Study Workbook on the Book of Ezra

Devotionals

How To Find Your Gratitude Attitude

Draw Closer 52-Week Devotional Journal

Praying Your Way Through Social Media: Reflections for Christian Artists and Entrepreneurs (collaboration with Latasha Strachan)

God Sees You: 21 Devotions for the Woman Who Feels Invisible

The Battle Is Not Yours: 21 Devotions for Spiritual Warfare

God Is In Control: 21 Devotions on God's Sovereignty

For Teens

Royal: Lessons from the Book of Esther

Learn more about my books at https://tinyurl.com/ACooteBooks

Free Gift Offer

Don't you wish you had the courage to face your fears? To choose faith over fear? Victory rather than defeat?

This short e-book will challenge the way you think about fear by identifying what fear is and why you need to eradicate it.

Tackle some of the most common fears like:

- Fear of inadequacy
- Fear of rejection
- Fear of missing out.

Draw power from the Bible verses provided to help you face down each fear with faith. You can face your fears.

Join Aminata's newsletter at https://tinyurl.com/FaceFearEbook and get a free copy of the e-book *Face Your Fears*.

www.ingramcontent.com/pod-product-compliance
Lightning Source LLC
Chambersburg PA
CBHW070546160726
48003CB00005B/1915